This book belongs to:

Name: _______________________________

Address: _______________________________

____

Home #: _______________________________

Cell #: _______________________________

Email: _______________________________

Emergency Contacts:

Name: _______________________________

Cell#: _______________________________

Name: _______________________________

Cell#: _______________________________

Name: _______________________________

Cell#: _______________________________

Name: _______________________________

Cell#: _______________________________

January

1	Name	Event	Year

2	Name	Event	Year

3	Name	Event	Year

4	Name	Event	Year

5	Name	Event	Year

January

6	Name	Event	Year

7	Name	Event	Year

8	Name	Event	Year

9	Name	Event	Year

10	Name	Event	Year

January

11	Name	Event	Year

12	Name	Event	Year

13	Name	Event	Year

14	Name	Event	Year

15	Name	Event	Year

January

16	Name	Event	Year

17	Name	Event	Year

18	Name	Event	Year

19	Name	Event	Year

20	Name	Event	Year

January

21	Name	Event	Year

22	Name	Event	Year

23	Name	Event	Year

24	Name	Event	Year

25	Name	Event	Year

January

26	Name	Event	Year

27	Name	Event	Year

28	Name	Event	Year

29	Name	Event	Year

30	Name	Event	Year

January

	Name	Event	Year
31			

Notes:

____

____

____

____

____

____

____

____

____

____

February

1	Name	Event	Year

2	Name	Event	Year

3	Name	Event	Year

4	Name	Event	Year

5	Name	Event	Year

February

6	Name	Event	Year

7	Name	Event	Year

8	Name	Event	Year

9	Name	Event	Year

10	Name	Event	Year

February

11	Name	Event	Year

12	Name	Event	Year

13	Name	Event	Year

14	Name	Event	Year

15	Name	Event	Year

February

16	Name	Event	Year

17	Name	Event	Year

18	Name	Event	Year

19	Name	Event	Year

20	Name	Event	Year

February

21	Name	Event	Year

22	Name	Event	Year

23	Name	Event	Year

24	Name	Event	Year

25	Name	Event	Year

February

26	Name	Event	Year

27	Name	Event	Year

28	Name	Event	Year

29	Name	Event	Year

Notes:

____

____

March

1	Name	Event	Year

2	Name	Event	Year

3	Name	Event	Year

4	Name	Event	Year

5	Name	Event	Year

March

6	Name	Event	Year

7	Name	Event	Year

8	Name	Event	Year

9	Name	Event	Year

10	Name	Event	Year

March

	Name	Event	Year
11			

	Name	Event	Year
12			

	Name	Event	Year
13			

	Name	Event	Year
14			

	Name	Event	Year
15			

March

16	Name	Event	Year

17	Name	Event	Year

18	Name	Event	Year

19	Name	Event	Year

20	Name	Event	Year

March

21	Name	Event	Year

22	Name	Event	Year

23	Name	Event	Year

24	Name	Event	Year

25	Name	Event	Year

March

26	Name	Event	Year

27	Name	Event	Year

28	Name	Event	Year

29	Name	Event	Year

30	Name	Event	Year

March

31	Name	Event	Year

Notes:

April

1	Name	Event	Year

2	Name	Event	Year

3	Name	Event	Year

4	Name	Event	Year

5	Name	Event	Year

April

6	Name	Event	Year

7	Name	Event	Year

8	Name	Event	Year

9	Name	Event	Year

10	Name	Event	Year

April

	Name	Event	Year
11			

	Name	Event	Year
12			

	Name	Event	Year
13			

	Name	Event	Year
14			

	Name	Event	Year
15			

April

16	Name	Event	Year

17	Name	Event	Year

18	Name	Event	Year

19	Name	Event	Year

20	Name	Event	Year

April

21	Name	Event	Year

22	Name	Event	Year

23	Name	Event	Year

24	Name	Event	Year

25	Name	Event	Year

April

26	Name	Event	Year

27	Name	Event	Year

28	Name	Event	Year

29	Name	Event	Year

30	Name	Event	Year

May

	Name	Event	Year
1			

	Name	Event	Year
2			

	Name	Event	Year
3			

	Name	Event	Year
4			

	Name	Event	Year
5			

May

6	Name	Event	Year

7	Name	Event	Year

8	Name	Event	Year

9	Name	Event	Year

10	Name	Event	Year

May

11	Name	Event	Year

12	Name	Event	Year

13	Name	Event	Year

14	Name	Event	Year

15	Name	Event	Year

May

16	Name	Event	Year

17	Name	Event	Year

18	Name	Event	Year

19	Name	Event	Year

20	Name	Event	Year

May

21	Name	Event	Year

22	Name	Event	Year

23	Name	Event	Year

24	Name	Event	Year

25	Name	Event	Year

May

26	Name	Event	Year

27	Name	Event	Year

28	Name	Event	Year

29	Name	Event	Year

30	Name	Event	Year

May

31	Name	Event	Year

Notes:

____

____

____

____

____

____

____

____

____

____

____

June

1	Name	Event	Year

2	Name	Event	Year

3	Name	Event	Year

4	Name	Event	Year

5	Name	Event	Year

June

6	Name	Event	Year

7	Name	Event	Year

8	Name	Event	Year

9	Name	Event	Year

10	Name	Event	Year

June

11	Name	Event	Year

12	Name	Event	Year

13	Name	Event	Year

14	Name	Event	Year

15	Name	Event	Year

June

16	Name	Event	Year

17	Name	Event	Year

18	Name	Event	Year

19	Name	Event	Year

20	Name	Event	Year

June

21	Name	Event	Year

22	Name	Event	Year

23	Name	Event	Year

24	Name	Event	Year

25	Name	Event	Year

June

26	Name	Event	Year

27	Name	Event	Year

28	Name	Event	Year

29	Name	Event	Year

30	Name	Event	Year

July

1	Name	Event	Year

2	Name	Event	Year

3	Name	Event	Year

4	Name	Event	Year

5	Name	Event	Year

July

6

Name	Event	Year

7

Name	Event	Year

8

Name	Event	Year

9

Name	Event	Year

10

Name	Event	Year

July

	Name	Event	Year
11			

	Name	Event	Year
12			

	Name	Event	Year
13			

	Name	Event	Year
14			

	Name	Event	Year
15			

July

16	Name	Event	Year

17	Name	Event	Year

18	Name	Event	Year

19	Name	Event	Year

20	Name	Event	Year

July

21	Name	Event	Year

22	Name	Event	Year

23	Name	Event	Year

24	Name	Event	Year

25	Name	Event	Year

July

26	Name	Event	Year

27	Name	Event	Year

28	Name	Event	Year

29	Name	Event	Year

30	Name	Event	Year

July

31	Name	Event	Year

Notes:

____

____

____

____

____

____

____

____

____

____

____

August

1	Name	Event	Year

2	Name	Event	Year

3	Name	Event	Year

4	Name	Event	Year

5	Name	Event	Year

August

6	Name	Event	Year

7	Name	Event	Year

8	Name	Event	Year

9	Name	Event	Year

10	Name	Event	Year

August

	Name	Event	Year
11			

	Name	Event	Year
12			

	Name	Event	Year
13			

	Name	Event	Year
14			

	Name	Event	Year
15			

August

16	Name	Event	Year

17	Name	Event	Year

18	Name	Event	Year

19	Name	Event	Year

20	Name	Event	Year

August

21	Name	Event	Year

22	Name	Event	Year

23	Name	Event	Year

24	Name	Event	Year

25	Name	Event	Year

August

26	Name	Event	Year

27	Name	Event	Year

28	Name	Event	Year

29	Name	Event	Year

30	Name	Event	Year

August

31	Name	Event	Year

Notes:

____

____

____

____

____

____

____

____

____

____

____

September

1	Name	Event	Year

2	Name	Event	Year

3	Name	Event	Year

4	Name	Event	Year

5	Name	Event	Year

September

6	Name	Event	Year

7	Name	Event	Year

8	Name	Event	Year

9	Name	Event	Year

10	Name	Event	Year

September

11	Name	Event	Year

12	Name	Event	Year

13	Name	Event	Year

14	Name	Event	Year

15	Name	Event	Year

September

16	Name	Event	Year

17	Name	Event	Year

18	Name	Event	Year

19	Name	Event	Year

20	Name	Event	Year

September

21	Name	Event	Year

22	Name	Event	Year

23	Name	Event	Year

24	Name	Event	Year

25	Name	Event	Year

September

26	Name	Event	Year

27	Name	Event	Year

28	Name	Event	Year

29	Name	Event	Year

30	Name	Event	Year

October

1	Name	Event	Year

2	Name	Event	Year

3	Name	Event	Year

4	Name	Event	Year

5	Name	Event	Year

October

6	Name	Event	Year

7	Name	Event	Year

8	Name	Event	Year

9	Name	Event	Year

10	Name	Event	Year

October

11	Name	Event	Year

12	Name	Event	Year

13	Name	Event	Year

14	Name	Event	Year

15	Name	Event	Year

October

16	Name	Event	Year

17	Name	Event	Year

18	Name	Event	Year

19	Name	Event	Year

20	Name	Event	Year

October

	Name	Event	Year
21			

	Name	Event	Year
22			

	Name	Event	Year
23			

	Name	Event	Year
24			

	Name	Event	Year
25			

October

26	Name	Event	Year

27	Name	Event	Year

28	Name	Event	Year

29	Name	Event	Year

30	Name	Event	Year

October

31	Name	Event	Year

Notes:

____

____

____

____

____

____

____

____

____

____

November

1	Name	Event	Year

2	Name	Event	Year

3	Name	Event	Year

4	Name	Event	Year

5	Name	Event	Year

November

6	Name	Event	Year

7	Name	Event	Year

8	Name	Event	Year

9	Name	Event	Year

10	Name	Event	Year

November

11	Name	Event	Year

12	Name	Event	Year

13	Name	Event	Year

14	Name	Event	Year

15	Name	Event	Year

November

16	Name	Event	Year

17	Name	Event	Year

18	Name	Event	Year

19	Name	Event	Year

20	Name	Event	Year

November

21	Name	Event	Year

22	Name	Event	Year

23	Name	Event	Year

24	Name	Event	Year

25	Name	Event	Year

November

26	Name	Event	Year

27	Name	Event	Year

28	Name	Event	Year

29	Name	Event	Year

30	Name	Event	Year

December

1	Name	Event	Year

2	Name	Event	Year

3	Name	Event	Year

4	Name	Event	Year

5	Name	Event	Year

December

6	Name	Event	Year

7	Name	Event	Year

8	Name	Event	Year

9	Name	Event	Year

10	Name	Event	Year

December

11	Name	Event	Year

12	Name	Event	Year

13	Name	Event	Year

14	Name	Event	Year

15	Name	Event	Year

December

16	Name	Event	Year

17	Name	Event	Year

18	Name	Event	Year

19	Name	Event	Year

20	Name	Event	Year

December

21	Name	Event	Year

22	Name	Event	Year

23	Name	Event	Year

24	Name	Event	Year

25	Name	Event	Year

December

26	Name	Event	Year

27	Name	Event	Year

28	Name	Event	Year

29	Name	Event	Year

30	Name	Event	Year

December

	Name	Event	Year
31			

Notes:

____

____

____

____

____

____

____

____

____

____

____